Isaac and Rebekah

Genesis 24 for Children

Written by Anna Logan
Illustrated by Susan Morris

ARCH® Books
Copyright © 1990
Concordia Publishing House
3558 S. Jefferson Avenue, St. Louis, MO 63118-3968
Manufactured in the United States of America

Sad Abraham was worried.
   He'd lived a long, long life.
And now the time had come to find
   His youngest son a wife.

He called his servant to him,
     "My son is now a man.
Go find a wife for Isaac
     To carry out God's plan.

"She must not live in Canaan,
     For Isaac needs a bride
Who comes from my own people
     To stay right by his side."

While Isaac sat and wondered,
"What will my bride be like?"
The worried servant started out,
His camels loaded high.

When evening came he rested
    Beside a well near town.
He did not know which girl to pick
    And knelt down on the ground.

"Dear God," he prayed, "please help me.
    I don't know what to think.
Please tell the bride for Isaac,
    My camels need a drink!"

Before he finished praying,
    Rebekah came in view.
The thirsty servant asked her,
    "May I get water from you?"

"Of course," Rebekah answered.
    "Your camels need help, too.
I'll get more water quickly
    And watch them till they're through."

"Hurray!" the servant shouted.
    "Here's gold and gifts for you.
Please take me to your family
    And let me meet them, too."

"Dear God," he prayed, "I thank You,
    You led me to this place.
You sent Rebekah to me
    And blessed her with Your grace."

(But back at home poor Isaac
    Still thought about the plan
And did not know the servant
    Was now a happy man!)

"Please stay all night," said Laban.
"There's lots of food to eat.
I'll give your camels hay and straw
And wash your tired feet!"

Rebekah told her family
    The joyful servant's news.
And then her brother Laban
    Went out to meet him, too.

The servant said, "Please listen.
    I must tell why I've come.
For Abraham has sent me
    And God's will must be done.

"Rebekah must come with me,
    For God has heard me pray.
She is the bride for Isaac.
    Please send her on her way."

"This is God's will," said Laban.
  "Of course, we'll let her go!"
Rebekah said good-bye to them
  And started down the road.

The servant walked beside her.
  His worries now were gone.
He'd looked to God for guidance,
  And God's good will was done.

As Isaac watched one evening,
    In a field outside his home,
He saw the camels walking
    And knew his bride had come.

Rebekah married Isaac—
    A very happy man!
And God blessed them with children
    According to His plan.

Dear Parents,

In this story we focus on the worry of Abraham's servant as he attempts to obey Abraham's command to find a suitable wife for his son Isaac. Discuss with your child times when you have worried and tried to handle problems yourself, rather than bringing them to God.

In Gen. 24:14, the servant asks God for a sign. He knows he is dependent on God's guidance, and God answers his prayer before he even finishes speaking. Rebekah comes to the well and offers water to both the servant and his camels as he had requested in his prayer. Assure your child that God hears every prayer and answers our needs before we even speak them.

Note that in Gen. 24:50, Rebekah's father, Bethuel, and brother Laban accept Abraham's plan as God's will. They don't even think about Rebekah's leaving home from their own point of view. They respond to God's leading in faithful obedience. Isaac and Rebekah marry according to God's plan.

Try listing some family decisions that can involve your child. Pray together and ask God for guidance, knowing He will give you firm direction.

The Editor